ALSO BY N. SCOTT MOM

Earth Keeper: Reflections on the American Land

The Death of Sitting Bear: New and Selected Poems

Again the Far Morning: New and Selected Poems

Three Plays: The Indolent Boys, Children of the Sun, and The Moon in Two Windows

Four Arrows & Magpie: A Kiowa Story

In the Bear's House

The Man Made of Words: Essays, Stories, Passages

Circle of Wonder: A Native American Christmas Story

In the Presence of the Sun: Stories and Poems, 1961–1991

The Ancient Child

The Names: A Memoir

The Gourd Dancer

Angel of Geese and Other Poems

The Way to Rainy Mountain

House Made of Dawn

The Journey of Tai-me

DREAM DRAWINGS

Configurations of a Timeless Kind

N. SCOTT MOMADAY

Illustrations by the author

HARPER ⬤ PERENNIAL

NEW YORK • LONDON • TORONTO • SYDNEY • NEW DELHI • AUCKLAND

HARPER ● PERENNIAL

HarperCollins books may be purchased for educational, business, or
sales promotional use. For information please email the Special Markets
Department at SPsales@harpercollins.com.

FIRST EDITION

All artwork by N. Scott Momaday

Designed by Jamie Lynn Kerner

Library of Congress Cataloging-in-Publication Data

Names: Momaday, N. Scott, 1934- author.
Title: Dream drawings : configurations of a timeless kind / N. Scott
   Momaday ; illustrations by the author.
Description: First edition. | New York : Harper Perennial, [2022] |
Identifiers: LCCN 2021058432 (print) | LCCN 2021058433 (ebook) | ISBN
   9780063218116 (trade paperback) | ISBN 9780063218123 (ebook)
Subjects: LCSH: Prose poems, American. | LCGFT: Prose poems.
Classification: LCC PS3563.O47 D74 2022 (print) | LCC PS3563.O47 (ebook)
   | DDC 811/.54—dc23/eng/20211215
LC record available at https://lccn.loc.gov/2021058432
LC ebook record available at https://lccn.loc.gov/2021058433

22 23 24 25 26 LSC 10 9 8 7 6 5 4 3 2

For Jacqueline

CONTENTS

PREFACE

According to the late writer and scientist Lewis Thomas, language was invented by children who came together thousands of years ago and played all day long. At the end of that day, we had language. This seems to me quite a plausible theory, and I have seen the validation of it in my own children.

Language is magical. Nothing in our world has been so instrumental in determining the history of our species. When we speak or read or write we are transformed into an intelligence made of words. It is our human being. We became human when we acquired language.

Language and the imagination work hand in hand, and together they enable us to reveal us to ourselves in story. That is indeed a magical process, and it is the foundation of art and literature.

We imagine and we dream, and we translate our dreams into language. This book is an enactment of that creative process. It is a celebration of words for their own sake.

N. Scott Momaday

DREAM DRAWINGS

THE ORIGINAL STORYTELLER

I could tell you a story.

I could tell you a story without words.

I could look you a story in the eyes.

You would understand the story,

Or you would feel more than understand the story.

It would be the story of my life.

It would be a story within a story.

The story would contain only interesting things.

It would not be less than a whole story.

You would hear the story in my silence.

The story would make you laugh and cry.

Well then, I would tell you a story.

ON DREAMING

From this reality my words become,
And I am left to calculate the sum
Of meaning. Rather would I gather dreams
And find in dreaming more than meaning seems.

CENTAUR

The boy caught sight of the animal as it grazed in a cover of grasses. It was a bright morning in the story of time. It might have been yesterday or thousands of years ago. The boy caught his breath. Never had he seen, or even dreamed, of such a creature. Latent, it seemed a work of art, a statue or a painting on a cave wall, perhaps. It was equal to the far reach of the boy's wonder. The boy shouted in pure delight, and the animal erupted in motion. It ran at great speed, and the strength that informed its whole body was under perfect control. Light rippled on its flanks, its blue-black hooves struck like rapid drumbeats on the earth, and its chiseled head lunged like the point of a spear into the crystal air. Tears came to the boy's eyes, and in his mind there came a conviction that he could barely express: We belong to each other, this creature and I.

TO HOLD THE SUN

An old man of no use walked in the plain. He was lost in his mind. He caught a splinter of the sun and held it in his hands. He had forgotten, but at that moment he remembered, who he was.

THE SCOP

My imagination turns upon words. I am certain that I was there in the forest when a storyteller recited *Beowulf* to a gathering of villagers in Anglo-Saxon England, common folk for whom such a performance was magical. And I have heard the thunder of King Lear's voice on the boards of the Globe Theatre in Elizabethan London. I was spellbound. Emily Dickinson read to me a poem she had written about crickets in which she realized a precision of statement that defies description. Czeslaw Milosz read his magnificent "Esse" to an audience in Ohio. I was there. I know these voices as well as I know my own, for I have heard them in my dreams. Dreams are the language of the imagination, and words are the conceptual symbols of our dreams. The scop, the actor, the writer, the storyteller draw with words. All of human history and all that can be dreamed of the future is contained in such drawings. I hear ancient voices striving for meaning and art, and I see crude and beautiful images on the walls of caves. *Deo gratias.*

THE SPIRITUAL GRAVITY OF PLACE

There are places in the world that lay claim to you, though you have been to them only once or not at all. They are places that you know imperfectly in your recollection or unaccountably in your dreams. Once, I visited the ancient city of Samarkand. I was there a few days, but it seems to me that I lived there throughout some years of my life. There I stepped out of time and into the vortex of cellular memory. Samarkand absorbed my whole being. And in my dreams I have come to Tintagel, or rather the mythic city of Camelot, which holds for me the same spiritual gravity. I have been there, though I have not, and there I have heard someone say, "Ah, you have returned. Welcome!"

THE REALIZATION OF NOTHING

At Brocéliande I joined a group of sightseers at Merlin's tomb. Their guide was a portly man of average aspect who looked to be in his fifties or sixties. His eyebrows and beard were white, and there was an air of sagacity about him. He proclaimed himself a Druid, and he spoke of Merlin with great authority. He held easily and securely the attention of his audience. There was something unusual about him. I felt that he existed in a separate age, a dimension of experience quite apart from my own. When he finished his remarks I approached him, told him that I had never met a Druid, and asked him if I might take his picture. He very kindly agreed. But when I held the camera to my eye I could not find him in the viewfinder. Nevertheless I snapped the shutter. Later, when I had the film developed, that was the only exposure on which there was no image at all. There was the realization of nothing.

GUESTS

At the dinner table what did I hear and see that evening?
An apparition? I wonder. It was so fleetingly visible, a man
followed by a dog. I heard the screen door through which
they entered slam shut, and they were inside. Immediately
they disappeared, not into thin air, as ghosts are said to do,
but into a room that was perhaps two steps away. In that
instant they were registered on my sight, a mere glimpse that
even now is there. After a moment of perplexity I asked the
woman seated next to me if she had seen them. She had not.
Indeed they were never to be seen again. In time I gave them
names, Christian Rood and his dog Sebastian. It is not for
me to question their existence. They were there, and I know
their names.

THE MOONLIGHT PASSAGE

His mother died on the night of a lunar eclipse. There was a radiant blue light on the world, and the heavens shimmered. The light of the moon had been important in her life. Her own mother had died in the influenza epidemic of 1918. How many times had his mother told him of an evening in her childhood? She remembered it as if it happened not eighty years but a day before. Her widowed father came home from work to find her upset and crying. He took her up in his arms and carried her outside. He placed her beside him in a surrey and took her for a ride. She was enthralled. The trees rustled above her, and the fields were bright and rolling, and she held the steady arm of her father. Never would she forget that moment. Now as she lay dying, her son leaned over her and whispered. He recollected for her that distant evening. He did not know if she heard him, but he imagined that his words bore her, as in a surrey on a moonlit country road, to the edge of her life and beyond, into a realm of childhood innocence and peace.

THE SPEECH

The words he spoke were few and for a time forgotten. When they were written down and published they were seen to be of profound merit. They expressed sentiments that were hidden in the hearts of men and women throughout the country, indeed throughout the world. They were committed to memory and recited even by children who did not entirely understand their meaning. They acquired the spirit of great literature. They became immortal. Had they not been preserved in writing, it is perhaps of no matter. They would surely have drifted like a swarm into the air and have been forever within our hearing in times of need.

TO MRS. CHARLES T. BUCKET OF
GREENFIELD, MASSACHUSETTS.

Charles Thomas Bucket dropped the shovel he had bought
from John Deere for two dollars. He entered the dark tent and
held a match to the wick of a kerosene lamp. Then he took up
the stub of a pencil and began a letter to his wife. "I have seen
the elephant," he wrote. It was all that need be written.

THE VISITORS

There was an evening service at the small country church, poorly attended because a storm had descended, and snow was falling. Pastor Anders preached a brief sermon on the subject of forgiveness. It was during the sermon that the three women entered the church and sat in the back pew. The pastor, who knew well the members of his congregation, had never seen these women before, and he thought it strange that they should appear out of nowhere on such a forbidding night. They were attentive, enclosed in silence, and they seemed remarkably alike, of the same mind and disposition. And then they left, as one, as if to keep an appointment at the center of darkness. Pastor Anders went directly to the door and looked out, thinking to bid them welcome, perhaps to offer assistance. But they had disappeared, and there were no footprints in the snow. There was only wonder and the profound isolation of the winter night.

THE CAPTURE

There is an eagle-hunt house among the cliffs, high above
the plain. It is a stone well built by the members of the eagle
hunters' society many years ago. I dreamed of going there as
a young man eager to make my name as a hunter. I carried
with me a leather bag, evergreen boughs and the fresh carcass
of a jackrabbit. I let myself down into the well and placed the
boughs over the opening, and on these I laid the rabbit. Then
I waited for a long time, crouched and uncomfortable. At last
the eagle came to take the rabbit, and as it touched the bait I
took hold of its legs and pulled it down into the well. There
was a terrible struggle. The wings of the great bird beat me
about the head and its talons tore into my hands and arms.
I managed to subdue the bird by placing the leather bag over
it, and I kept it alive. It would be kept in a cage in the village
as an emissary from its world. On the way down from the
cliffs I assumed the gait of a hunter.

THE CLOSE

The boy sat on the hillside waiting, watching with dread.
His eyes were fixed on the mouth of the cave below. Smoke
issued there, and the immediate sounds of battle, so fierce that
the boy trembled and could not look away. Then the dragon
appeared, its massive body slithering and its torn scales, each
one the size and shape of a shield, were iridescent as gems.
It roared, buckled violently, and lay still, its burning breath
extinguished. Then came forth the king, an old man mortally
wounded. A delirium seized him as he tried to speak but could
not. He tried one last time to raise his sword, but his scorched
arm was nearly severed, and he barely remembered a night in
his prime when he had torn Grendel's arm from his monstrous
body. For a mere moment the aura of glory shone about his
head, and he slumped to the ground. The boy wept.

THE DARK AMUSEMENT OF BEARS

Bears are amused by the concept of reality. They sit around imagining they are real, and they laugh.

THE SHADOW OF A NAME

The name Benevides came down from generation to generation. In time it landed on one Diego, a plain man who dreamed of his ancestors, those Conquistadors who came from Spain to the New World centuries ago. In his imagination they were heroic adventurers and soldiers of fortune, men of singular destiny and opportunity. He had neither of these things to speak of. Rather, he had only the realm of dreams and a life in the shadow of his ancestral name. In humility he accepted these blessings and, making the sign of the cross, took his place in the long procession of souls and in good faith.

LANDSCAPE WITH CLOUDS

In the foreground are scattered bushes on red earth. In the background are blue mountains beneath a bank of gray and white clouds. There is the hint of a summer storm. In the middle distance are a woman and a child walking on a dirt road. Their shapes are small and barely defined. They walk close together and with a hint of purpose, as if to keep an appointment of some moment along the way. They approach a tree on the side of the road. For a moment they disappear behind the tree, and then the woman reappears, but not the child. The woman proceeds at the same pace, with a hint of purpose. She moves through the wide landscape in which a summer storm may be gathering.

THE BIRTHRIGHT

You come to me with an innocence that once was mine.
You too will have your innocence while it is original and
undiminished, and in that time I will care for you as you are
in your spirit, for you are a sacred being. I make you the gift
of certain promises. I will try with all my heart to show you
what is good and beautiful in our world. I will lead you on
walks along clear streams in meadows of wildflowers, and I
will see that you have stories and music for the pleasure and
enrichment of your mind and soul. I will show how precious
are the colors of early mornings and late afternoons. I will
encourage your natural love of children and animals, for they
share your innocence. I will nourish your instinct for wonder
and delight. I will teach you how to exist in your imagination,
for therein is the true story of yourself. And as long as I have
you in my care I will protect you from hurt. Please accept these
promises with my deepest love. They are your birthright.

A MANTRA

I walk along a street in the Financial District. There are many pedestrians, men and women in business attire, going in and out of office buildings, shops and restaurants. Their expressions are serious, purposeful, or else they chatter to each other and smile knowingly. They are of a kind, and they are where they ought to be. They are visibly successful. But there is one among them who moves against the grain. He is a homeless man, aimless and unwashed. Unaccountably we take notice of each other. I pause to look into a window, and he approaches me. I wish to avoid him, but he presses against me and places a crumpled bit of paper in my hand. He moves on and I read what is written on the paper: "Be still. Gather yourself. The storm rolls away, and there comes a clear dawn."

OBSERVATIONS

I have observed the whorls of geology on a canyon wall, a splinter of the sun at my window, the far end of time on the desert, a butterfly alighting on a leaf, an old man praying, sunrise on the Great Plains, ravens playing with a young fox, wind whipping the sea, the look of wonder on a child's face, a snowfield in moonlight, and a small blue stone. Why should I fear death?

OWNERSHIP

I lived in a house in a canyon. Great cliffs rose up on either side, and one of them, sheer, white and dun and rose-colored, was especially beautiful. When the slanting light of the afternoon sun ascended on the face of it, I was made to hold my breath. It is simply good to reside in the presence of such a thing. It sustains the spirit. There was a young man, a drifter, who worked for me one summer. We spoke of the cliff, and he said, "It belongs to me, I don't own it, but it's mine." I thought about this, and I came to see the wisdom in it. True ownership does not consist in titles and deeds. It is assumed by a claim made in the heart, and it is purchased with love and respect. The cliff is his, as it is mine.

SONG OF THE JOURNEY

From the cold we came, isn't it

With the hurt of hunger we came, isn't it

The northern sun was our god, isn't it

We entered the sun's house, isn't it

The southern sun was our god, isn't it

The prairie wind sang to us, isn't it

We are the real people at home

We are the real people at home

Isn't it

CONFIGURATIONS OF A TIMELESS KIND

When I met her she was a hundred years old, more or less. As a child she attended the last Kiowa Sun Dance in 1887. In a small voice she told me of that event, which was wonderful to her, and I could see that she had become suspended in her memory, transported to a beloved time. She spoke, without having to search her mind, of the camps, the people, and the intricacies of the dance. And as I listened to her I became aware of the extraordinary essence of time, as it defined *this* moment, this mysterious and immediate facet of itself. The old woman had entered a world that was exclusively hers, a world in which I did not exist. And yet we both inhabited the present. Or did we? What is the isolation that determines our lives? In some sense perhaps I too attended the dance.

BEAT THE DRUM SLOWLY

It was an ordinary night in Fort Sumner, quiet but for the muffled sound of voices in the Spanish language, wafting through the darkness in song and speech. Billy and I had ridden in from San Patricio, a ride of several days, and we were dog tired. Nonetheless Billy went off at once to visit his sweetheart, Paulita, and left me to doze under the summer moon. At midnight Billy grew hungry and went to the house of Paulita's brother, Pedro, to cut meat from a side of beef that hung on the porch. Then I heard the shot that killed Billy the Kid. It startled me, of course, but I think I had been expecting it, for Billy was an outlaw and a wanted man. But I knew him to be a boy, lonely and homeless. We rode together. Much of my story is contained in those three words, *We rode together.* There is nothing more to say, except this: I hear again the shot and see again vague shadows on the moonlit ground.

DREAMING BEAR SPEAKS

I speak. I have thought about the bear of my name many times. And yes, he dreams. He dreams of being. He dreams of what it is to be a bear. He is bold, and he knows of his great strength. He dreams of danger, of overcoming danger with courage and disdain. He dreams of meadows under the sun and of ripe berries bursting in his teeth. He dreams of bright waters and the darting of birds in the trees. He dreams of rolling thunder and the beat of rain. And perhaps he dreams of me dreaming of him. Surely he dreams of my frailty and the burdens of my mind, and it may be that he dreams of assuming my doubts and fears. He dreams of being me, of being human. And in my dreams of the bear I will him to stand away, to keep to the wilderness in which he is brave and beautiful and at peace. The bear and I dream of each other in our name. That is very good, isn't it?

MERGER

It is said that one can compare a grain of sand to the desert, or a drop of water to the ocean, but one cannot compare time and eternity. What could have inspired the poet Frederick Goddard Tuckerman to write, "the moments take hold of eternity"? It is a brilliant figure in literature, a figure in the balance of which lies an insoluble equation. It is an image that is not an image, for it cannot be seen. It might suggest ship lights taking hold of the fog or smoke dissolving among leaves, but these are at last wide of the mark. What can be determined is this: On a day in Greenfield, Massachusetts, more than a century ago, a poet strove with the concept of evanescence and the merger of time and timelessness. In one singular and profound expression he might seem to have achieved the inexpressible. It is a thing to ponder.

TIME AND ESSENCE

One night a woman dreamed—or was it not a dream—
that there was a presence outside her window. Alarmed, she
crept to the window and looked out. There was a column of
smoke revolving slowly, and a voice inside the column said,
"I have come for you. Hurry, time is of the essence." The
woman might have been greatly frightened, but she was of a
thoughtful nature, and it occurred to her that she might be
dreaming. She was emboldened, and she said, "Time is indeed
of the essence. Come for me an hour ago." The column of
smoke began rapidly to spin, and it dissolved into the night.

CHIVALRY

So, I prove to be worthy of the Queen's admiration. And certainly she is worthy of mine. Her hair is of a sheen one cannot imagine, and when the breeze touches it, it seems to lift mortality from her face and give to her whole aspect a vibrancy like the dance of rain upon water. Her eyes glow with the radiance of embers, and they express perfectly her lithe spirit. To look into her eyes is to discover a depth equal to the sky itself. Her skin is the candor of moonlight upon satin and her mouth the ineffable essence of desire. I could further describe her to my lust, but the thought of Arthur intrudes upon my reverie. Does he know my mind, hers? He inspires fear, for he is first a warrior, then a king. I perceive him as the ghost he will become, standing tall on the headland at Tintagel, his dark visage hooded and his grasp firm upon his mythic sword. There is a rude splendor about him. He is the king, *my* king. I see him there, and beyond him the sea of his destiny. The Queen is also mine, and I tremble under her spell. I venture between love and allegiance. In the maze of my affections I crave a balance. God grant it.

THE NIGHT DANCE

The man was lost. He had walked all day among the dunes, and he was very tired. It had been extremely hot in the day, but now that night had fallen it became cold. He became feverish, and he shivered and became disoriented. He kept walking. At some point he saw the light of fires in the distance, and with much effort he made his way to them and warmed himself. No one was there, but the fires were burning. The fires bordered a bare space at one end of which was a small round house made of mud and logs. As the moon reached its zenith, masked figures emerged from the house and began to dance in single file, chanting. The man was spellbound. The motion seemed perpetual and the chanting unintelligible. It echoed from another world, a world the man knew in his mind immediately and unaccountably. He knew that he had come upon a ceremony of the gods, that he was made a strange and unique gift of witness, and that nothing in his familiar world would ever be the same again. But at first light the man beheld nothing more than circles of ash on the ground.

A SPELL FOR SETTING OUT

Let us be on our way

On our way the dawns appearing

On our way the plains appearing

On our way the clouds appearing

On our way the hills appearing

On our way the waters appearing

There is goodness on our way

There is gladness on our way

There are stories on our way

On our way

AN ACT OF MERCY

In the late afternoon a man was returning to his camp in the woods, when he saw in his path a grizzly bear. The bear stood solidly in his way and did not move. The man did not know what to do, but after a full minute of this ominous encounter, he began to talk softly to the bear, telling it what he thought it might like to hear. He told it of the bear who saved a maiden in distress. He even told it two episodes from *Winnie-the-Pooh*, but the bear just regarded him with what appeared to be disdain and perhaps pity. Then the bear turned and departed. The man thanked God. The next day the man again returned to his camp, and he found it utterly destroyed, and again he thanked God.

THE WOMAN WHO HELD SWAY

A warrior of the Raven band brought home a woman. She was unlike the other women in the band. Her blood and bones were of a different source, and she demanded attention and respect. It was not long before she held a position of leadership among the women. The men resented and resisted her as long as they could, but then they too fell under her power. In time she instilled in the band a sense of pride and confidence, especially in the women, who had formerly been submissive and weak. When an enemy band came to make war, the Raven warriors fought fiercely and were victorious. In council the leader of the women said to her sisters, "You see how it is to be strong. Our men were more afraid of us than they were of the enemy. The Raven band is in good hands."

TO SPEAK OF NOTHING

It is a serious thing, nothing.
The notion confounds the mind
As wind confounds the sea.
A woman fixes words to a miracle,
A man describes himself to God.
The syllables amount to something,
But they are nothing to speak of.

THE MASK

The mask was the creation of an anthropologist at the University of Toronto, a specialist in human evolution. Based on his thorough study of ancient skulls, it was the likeness of a man who lived thirty thousand years ago. The anthropologist was greatly pleased with the mask. Every day he looked at it with growing admiration. He began to talk to it and imagined that it talked back. He even named it after himself. One day he placed the mask over his face and looked at the reflection in a mirror. He was astonished. The mask seemed to reveal more truly who he was than did his own face. From that time on he wore the mask everywhere and all the time, and no one noticed that it was a mask.

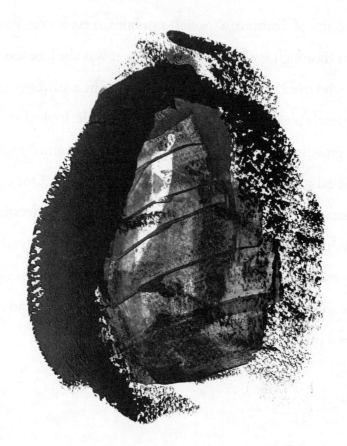

THE HOLLOW LOG

In very ancient times a tree grew up in an unknown place. Stories, too, must have grown up in that place, but they have been lost, or else they were beyond man's memory, embedded in the polar ice. The fragment of a story appears to have been recovered, and we can build upon it. The tree fell. In time nothing remained of it but a hollow log. Through the log our ancestors passed one by one into the present world. At this end of the log there were the things that define our world, meadows and mountains, rivers, and the sun and moon, altogether a rich and beautiful world. But what lay at the other end of the log? There is surely the realm of dreams, the place of the mind's marrow. It is the original place, the place of beginning. In the beginning were such words as these, and the foretelling of a story.

IN THE TELLING

The story does not end. Rather it revolves on a wheel of telling. It begins again. That is the way of story and storytelling; it is an endless way. In like manner, dreams do not end. They dissolve into infinite possibility. The story and the dream cannot be told apart. In the night I dreamed of a boy who turned into a bear. There is a story in that. Indeed there are many stories in the one. And indeed there is one story in the many. We roll on wheels of words and dreams.

THE WOMAN AT THE GLASS DOOR

No, not yet the door, though there is an after image,

Like the ghost of a monoprint. It is at a window

That she stands now, outside in the rain.

She looks in at me where I sit writing these lines.

Beside her a rose bush tumbles in the wind,

And a single yellow blossom bobs as if keeping time.

We nod to each other, and then she is gone.

I turn to the glass door and regard the transparent

Mask that remains of her having been a while ago,

Seeking some perspective on my loneliness.

ON THE IMAGINATION

From mere reality these words become
And we are left to calculate the sum.
But quest beyond reality and see
Into a corner of infinity.

PASSAGE

Then go

From these smoking hills

Through intervals of biding time,

And find solace in the going.

A stillness enfolds your moving shadow,

And your passage is made

Against a backdrop of ancient walls.

You are secure in the eagle's sight.

THE SHIELD THAT CAME HOME

Poor Buffalo dreamed that he was soon to die. He therefore spoke to his wife concerning his last wishes. "There is one thing above all," he said. "I want my shield to come home." Poor Buffalo's shield had been taken from him in battle some years before. The loss was a great sorrow to him. When he died, his wife with great effort found the shield and begged to have it returned, and so it was. There was a memorial service at which the shield was displayed. Poor Buffalo's wife spoke: "This shield is powerful, for it found a way to come home. It must be given our thanks and our respect, and it must always face the sun. The spirit of Poor Buffalo is alive in his shield." Cedar was burned and the people waved smoke upon themselves.

THE ZEBRA REPORT

A little girl swung in a swing. She pointed her toes and stretched her legs far out, and she swung higher and higher. She felt the air as she moved through it, and it seemed to her that the air too was moving, moving against her. It is a breeze of my very own making, she thought. *I* have made this breeze. It touches me, and it slips away. I have made a fine thing. And indeed the breeze did go on. It passed through the fence on the edge of the playground, rippled through Mabel Hodge's garden, curled about the steeple of the Methodist church, and gathered speed. It caught the sails of boats in the bay and whipped a froth upon the waves of the sea. It became a sandstorm in Africa and a tsunami on the coast of Japan. The little girl gave a report on zebras for her third-grade class.

THE MARROWBONE MANUSCRIPT

A farm boy, somewhat deficient in his mind, is said to have discovered the script, partially buried, on the side of a dirt road in 1910. The boy could not read, nor could those he let see it until it came into the hands of Pastor Nathan, a self-made man of the cloth who was literate. "This is the fragment of the epistle of Lucifer to Saint Isidore," he announced. "It proclaims the existence of a witch in our own neighborhood. We must beware, for it is written that she appears every seven years." The good people of Marrowbone were alarmed, the more so because no one knew when the next seventh year would fall. Then the farm boy suggested that perhaps the Marrowbone manuscript should be burned at the stake. And so it was. And there was a general relief.

A PROFOUND EVASION

"Is it tomorrow yet," the child inquired.
The question was unholy and inspired.
The keeper of the clocks contrived to say,
"I'm out of time, but ask me yesterday."

WITCHES

I had no time for skepticism. Witches accosted me from all directions. This is not an unusual circumstance for those who grow up in certain parts of the world. I grew up on American Indian reservations in the Southwest, where witches are entrenched in the culture and accepted as entitled members of the community. I know someone who proclaims herself a "white" witch, as opposed to a "black" witch, that is, one whose nature is benign; she does good deeds. In my experience most witches tend to be gray or black. They are mischief makers at best, and they can be dangerous. I like this about them. They sharpen our senses. They give a bit of salt to our diet. It is good that we have them among us, and it is good that we recognize, appreciate, and fear them. They deserve acknowledgment and respect, and they ought to inhabit some of our best stories.

THE ICE WOMAN

A whale hunter walked out into the night. There were shimmering colored lights in the night sky. They were so bright that they seemed to rend the darkness and set fire to the snowfields. The man was enchanted, and in his amazement and delight he began to whistle. Thereupon, one of the lights came down upon him like a bolt of lightning. It would surely have killed him, but the whale hunter was stronger than most men, and he seized the light and wrestled it to the ground. In his grasp the light became the frozen shape of a beautiful woman, an ice sculpture burning with brilliant colors from within. The ice woman continued to shimmer and writhe in the whale hunter's arms, and where she touched him he too turned to ice. His life was frozen in his bones. Everything the ice woman touched turned to ice, but it was not illumined by the bright dancing glow inside her, and she returned to the night sky.

THE VISIONS OF STONE CARRIER

Stone Carrier was my grandfather, my father, my brother, and my son. He was a good and brave man, and he taught me many things. He shared some of his memories with me, memories that were of another age than my own. Once, he told me of an encampment at Rainy Mountain. It was on the north side of the mountain, he said. It was a large camp, made up of many tepees, so many that they seemed a great flock of geese, come to pause in the course of their migration to the sun's winter house. I could see the camp in my mind's eye. It was the beautiful dream of a time that was cherished and lost. And on the east side of the mountain are the ruins of a boarding school that my grandmother attended as a child. Many years after it closed Stone Carrier would go there at night, and he could hear the voices of children sounding on the grass. There was laughter in the voices. And sometimes he could see smoke rising among the stars.

PAI-MAHTONE

She bore the sacred name of *Pai-mahtone*, Sun Woman, and she was indeed a sacred being. Her spirit was a brilliant reflection of the sun's light and warmth. It is said that her spirit will live as long as the sun lives, and she will never be forgotten. She was a great storyteller. It was she who told the story of Aila, who brought color to the world. You see, once there was only black and white in the world. The child Aila played by the river. She mixed sand and soil and leaves and grass with water, and she brushed the mixture upon the plane of the things about her—the trees, the rocks, the hills, everything. And where she brushed there emerged radiant bands of color. From that time on, the earth has been touched with beauty. And in telling the story of Aila, Pai-mahtone has given to her people the splendor of the sun.

THE SHAPE SHIFTER

In a dream I saw the young hunter Talilingua. He was dressed in polar bear skins, and he carried a harpoon. He was a renowned hunter, and he was in the prime of his life. He was running, and he seemed godlike. I watched him, full of admiration. He ran into a bank of fog and disappeared. I ran after him, determined to see him again, for the mere sight of him inspired me. But I could not find him. What I found was an ancient man, shriveled and blind, sitting cross-legged on the beach. He held an ivory story knife in his hand, and he was carving a story on a plane of snow. In my dream I could read his script, "I am Talilingua, the hunter."

BELIEF

I found that I believed in your belief.
You led me through the maze of joy and grief,
And somewhere in the emptiness of time
Belief became my weapon and my crime.

ON HORSEBACK HE SINGS

Of white and yellow stars
His riding song. Beyond the earth
His riding song. Of colored sands
His riding song. Beads of light
Flicker in his riding song.
They pulse on a dark blue field,
The very color of the velvet
His lover wore when they danced
On the canyon floor at Wide Water.
Happily he rides, happily he sings
His riding song. And happily
He will sleep beneath the stars
In the velvet sky as he dreams
His riding song. *Hozhoni.*

THE INSTRUMENT

You curtsy and beguile,
You place the bow and smile.
The cello sounds lament;
Such is the instrument
You hold in your embrace.
Solace cannot displace
The vibrancy of strings,
The hum of beating wings.
Yet sadness comprehends
The notes that solace sends.
No rhythms of discord
Will your grave play afford.
But give us this and more;
Be solemn the encore.

ALEXANDER AND BUCEPHALUS

There is a story told in the camps: In a well-attended ceremony, King Philip of Macedonia was presented with a fine horse. But when he tried to mount the animal, it bolted away. King Philip was angered and humiliated. Then his twelve-year-old son, Alexander, ran up to his father and asked if he might try to calm the horse. The boy noticed that the horse had shied from its own shadow, and he turned it towards the sun and mounted it easily. Philip was so impressed with his son's deed that he gave him the horse, which Alexander named Bucephalus, and on the back of Bucephalus, Alexander conquered much of the known world.

THE POET'S MUSE

She came to him as an apparition, a figure in a dream. He did
not know what she was at first, and he tried to name her, to
give her an acceptable definition, but nothing he could think
of caught her essence, and she was indeed essential. He was
perplexed. What was she that she could not be seen, touched,
revealed to his senses? She seemed to consist in air or mist or
silence. There were times when she seemed not to be at all. Yet
he knew of her being. She existed in some dimension apart
from reality. She was perhaps an extension of his imagination.
He thought that he might have invented her, but no, she was
beyond his influence. But he was not beyond hers. In her
means and vibrancy she gave him inspiration. She enabled him
to write well, to imagine himself as he imagined her, in words
that were informed with perception, precision, and truth. She
enabled him to accomplish his potential. Then one day, on a
street named Calle sin Nombre she appeared before him in
her corporeal guise. It was as if he had expected her for many
years. And on the surface of his mind he wrote *Thank You.*

THE HAT

Meir was a New Yorker. He loved the theater and became a successful playwright. He was devoted to the cinema, and he built a most impressive film library. He had never been to the American West, but he dreamed of it. Then his dream came true. He was invited to a writers' conference in Wyoming. His excitement was intense, and it grew nearly boundless when he entered the small, rustic town. It seemed a movie set. That evening he ventured out on the main street and imagined a gunfight in front of the livery stable. Then, his heart pounding, he entered the Big Horn saloon. It was smoky, loud, and favored by painted ladies and men in boots and ten-gallon hats. Meir sat down. At the adjoining table was an authentic cowboy. After a few minutes the cowboy removed his hat, placed it carefully on the table, and went to the men's room. Meir, full of curiosity, could not help going over and picking up the hat. The bartender came at once and said, "Around here we don't touch a man's hat." The cowboy returned and said to the contrite Meir, "Aw, hell, that's all right, you didn't know."

THE SHOUT

He was a child among children. Together they formed a critical mass. Indeed, they seemed the first inhabitants of the first world. They played all day long, running, skipping, tumbling, shouting. It was in their shouting that they changed the world. It was he, especially, who was responsible, for he shouted the sound that became a word. Had he known, he might have been struck dumb. But he repeated the sound again and again. The others took it up, and at last it carried into meaning, and it became the stream of language. It was the origin of human being. Thereafter the child had a recurrent dream, and the word, the original word, reverberated in his mind and multiplied. Words enabled him to think, and thoughts informed his dreams. He dreamed of children at play in a former world.

THE MEADOW

Jacqueline

There is a meadow.
It is a place of grasses
Whispering of rain,
Of bluebells and buttercups.
I will meet you there
In summer when a music
Drifts among the hills.

There is a meadow,
A saucer of the green earth.
I will meet you there
When clouds lay moving shadows
On the rolling plain.
Among the distant mountains
Is the smoke of dreams.

There is a meadow.

In the surround of seasons,

In the turn of time

And memories of delight,

I will meet you there,

And we will touch our being

To the velvet wind.

There is a meadow.

On a carpet of colors

I will meet you there.

THE OCTOPUS DREAMING

Once I found an octopus stranded on a beach. I thought
it was dead, but when I touched it with a bit of driftwood,
it suddenly changed color, from gray to a deep violet. The
transformation startled me, for it was entirely unexpected and
it seemed a profound emergence of life, a bursting forth of
some otherworldly and irresistible energy that was unknown
to me. This strange encounter made an indelible impression
on my mind, a kind of cornerstone of the memory. I have since
heard it speculated, on the basis of scientific investigation, that
an octopus changes color according to its dreams. I dreamed
of my octopus, and I dare say it might well have dreamed
of me. What color or colors might I have inspired in the
creature's dreams? I hope I might have appeared to it as a blue
abstraction, interesting if not beautiful, stranded on a littoral
of the imagination.

ARFIG THE WITCH

He visited exotic places on the earth, places he could not have imagined, and he encountered people who were strange to him. In general, he got on well enough with them, even though they spoke different languages and had different customs and views of the world. Once, on Greenland, at the original Thule, he chanced upon a woman (or was she?) he would remember as long as he lived. In the small Inuit village, the only accommodation he could find was at the old people's home. One night as he walked in the hallway he passed by an open door, and he glanced in. There, sitting on her bed, was an ancient creature looking at him. Her eyes were holes of black liquid, and her expression, to the extent there was one, seemed malicious. He passed quickly by, but he felt a rush of cold air from her room. When later he asked about her, he was told that she was Arfig the witch and that she had died in the room many years before.

THE EXPLORER

There came a knock on my door late at night. Who could be calling? It was midwinter, and the weather was extremely cold. I opened the door, and there stood a small man, and behind him a dog team and a sledge. He seemed very weak and tired. I ushered him in, sat him down before my fire, and gave him hot tea. I learned that he was a famous explorer, then making the longest dog-team journey ever attempted. He was cordial and altogether willing to answer my questions. I asked him what had been the most difficult part of his trek so far. "Oh, Baffin Island. It was cold, desolate, dark, lonely. I don't think I could have made it if it had not been for the fish." After a long pause, I dared to ask, "Fish, what fish?" He replied at once, "There were piles of fish along the way, enough to feed me and my dogs." There was another silence, and I asked, "Where did the fish come from?" And in the manner of one who has witnessed a miracle, he replied, "The bears, the bears set out the fish for me." There was such wonder and conviction in his voice I had no recourse but to believe him.

PRINTS

So many prints have I left in the sand,

I look back, and age clouds my vision,

And memory is no longer true. Was it you

Who spoke the words that I hear now,

Or do I hear the wind? There are echoes.

Did we see eagles hold still in the clouds

Above the hills of Umbria? Were we there,

You and I? I would walk with you again

Among the groves and hedges, the houses

Drawn with pastels on a plane of sunlight.

I would know again the precise touch,

The mere impression of your hand in mine.

Did the moon shine on trellises of leaves

Where we sat over *biscotti* and *vin santo*?

Do I now inhabit a dream of these things?

On my crooked way are prints in the sand.

There is a glitter on the smoldering path

And the burn of loss in the vagrant mind.

A DREAM OF BECOMING OLD

He lived alone in the woods. It was impossible to say how old he was, only that he had lived a very long time. He told me this story: "When I was a young man I saw a child playing in the grass. She was happy, and her happiness was contagious. I could not help going up to her. 'What are you doing,' I asked. 'I am having tea with my grandmother,' she replied. 'But I do not see your grandmother,' I said. 'Where is she?' 'She is here in my dream; she tells me stories.' I was intrigued. 'May I join you in your dream?' 'Please, please come in.' I sat beside her grandmother, who was charming and lively. She told a story of unicorns. Then the three of us held hands and made a circle of wonder. You know, in the dream I grew old. It seemed I was on a pilgrimage through time. And as it should be, time was both lost and gained. I came away the same, yet a profoundly changed man. It was a graceful and appropriate transformation. I shall always remember and be thankful for that day, the day I entered the dream of a child."

A STROKE UPON THE EARTH

The tree was very old and a part of it had turned to stone. A few minutes after noon the old man emerged from the shadow of the tree. He was seen by a boy who had been waiting and watching. The boy approached the old man and said, "I saw a woman and a child approach on the road and disappear behind the tree. A moment later the woman appeared but the child did not. And now it is you who appears. Can you explain to me what happened, for I cannot believe my eyes." The old man replied, "My mother and I were walking to San Ysidro. We were hot and thirsty and tired. When we came to the tree we stopped to rest in the shade. I was very young, and the heat of the sun had weakened me. 'You must stay here and rest until your strength returns,' my mother said, 'then follow me. I will find a well with cool water in San Ysidro. Meet me there.' I waited in the shade of the tree. At high noon there came a stroke upon the earth. Time became a whirlwind in the shadow, and at its center a profound stasis, as if in the split moment the world had come to an end, only to begin again. And in that strange nick of time I grew old. And now I must go to my mother. She waits for me at the well."

MISS O'KEEFFE OF ABIQUIU

She was in her mind and art a woman of the landscape, and
her landscape was that of northern New Mexico—Ghost
Ranch, Abiquiu, Santa Fe. I met her on a cold February day
at her home in Abiquiu. She was then in her eighties, and her
eyesight was failing. Even so, she continued to paint, and her
later work was worthy of her prime. She was, and is, among
the world's great artists. I was familiar with her work, but
it was not until I sat across from her in conversation that I
discerned the true nature of her character and her genius. We
became friends, and on a number of occasions I brought wine
and cheese, and we told each other stories. I wanted especially
to know what she saw when she looked into the landscape, *her*
landscape, for it was mine too. I had lived much of my life in
it, and I knew that it was incomparable to both of us. The land
was our bond. On the day Georgia O'Keeffe died I was giving
a reading of my poems at Bucknell University. I included, in
memoriam, the poem "Forms of the Earth at Abiquiu," which
I wrote for her soon after our first meeting. I trust she heard it.

THE WHISPERER

There was a spilling moon. The window was open, and the curtains billowed in a soft breeze. The woman breathed in a rhythm of unrest. She was neither asleep nor awake. The words came in a whisper. She listened, straining to hear, but the voice was very low, and the words were nearly unintelligible. She thought she heard a name, "Andrew . . ." Suddenly she was wide awake. Andrew was her brother's name. He had fought and died in Vietnam. All day she fretted and moved aimlessly through the rooms of the house. She paused again and again at the window in her bedroom. Had she really heard her brother's voice? Much later she confided to a friend, "After that night I could no longer mourn, for I knew that in some undeniable way Andrew was alive. He was there, and he had a voice." She did not hear the voice again, but on nights of the spilling moon she felt her brother's presence nearby.

THE DEATH OF BEAUTY

Thirty men attended her funeral. Each one of them was grief-stricken. Mary Worthington died as she had lived, dreary and alone. She was born to sorrow, her mother said, and those who knew her agreed. She seemed to have no confidence in herself, no hope for the future. Even as a child, she kept to the dark corners of her world and did not show herself to others. She lived her life in this reclusive way. She did not know that she was beautiful, one of the most beautiful women of all. But some knew, and they were heard to comment. She gained the reputation of a most desirable creature. Men came calling, but they were turned away. She continued to live in loneliness, but at the end of her life she came to understand that she had been beautiful and that she might have had a claim to happiness. Thirty men wept and said it was so.

TRANSPARENCY

In those days the man drove a wagon thirty miles to buy goods
from a trading post. The way was rough, but if the weather was
favorable, he could cover the distance in one day, the round
trip in two. On this day however, there was a heavy snow, and
the horses could not go at their usual pace. Night was coming
on, and the man set up a camp. He hobbled the horses and
built a fire. Then, protected from the cold, he went to sleep.
Something woke him, and he peered into the darkness. There
on the edge of the firelight was a bear. Strangely the man was
not frightened. He took a step towards the bear, then another,
and another. The bear, with no perceptible motion of its body,
kept the same distance from the man. Then the bear seemed to
become diaphanous, as if the moon had cast a clear film upon
it. And through this strange transparency the man saw a wolf.
The wolf was bewildered and ran away. The man thereafter
believed that the bear had been sent to save him from the wolf.
This story he told to the village priest, but the priest did not
believe him.

SHADOW

His spirit belonged to the night and the moon. The brighter
the moon the better, he thought. As a boy, he had taken
great delight in the moon. He waited each day for the night
to come. Then he went out to look for the moon. When he
saw it, and the light it cast on the world, he was exhilarated.
And when he saw that he made a shadow on the moonlit
ground, he was beside himself with joy. *Beside himself* indeed.
His shadow cleaved to him. So long as the moon shone, his
shadow was an extension of his being. He began to think of
it as a companion, steady and true. But as the years went by
his beloved shadow grew dim and disappeared. Artificial light
poured on him from every direction, and his shadow was
confused and diminished. He looked for the soft, constant
image of himself, but it had been obliterated by the ubiquitous
glare of artificial light. The moon, and indeed the night itself,
had been made less available to his eye and his imagination.
The man mourned the loss of his shadow and something of his
spirit. He dreamed of a moon in Genesis.

PRAYER TO THE SUN

O Great Deity, I sing this prayer in your praise. Hear my
honor song! My words quiver in your presence. You appear
each day on the dark rim. You rise in water and you set in
fire. You touch a brilliance to the hills, and they smolder. You
clarify the plain, and you make crystalline the wind. You
lay seams across the mountains. They are ribbons of azure
in the dawn, and they are pools of umber in the dusk. Your
burning blinds me, and yet you give me to see beauty in all
the corners of Creation. I will sing the glory of your radiance,
and my breath will become that of the eagle that hies above
the meadows and cries the mystical center of your being. In
devotion I sing, and my feet strike the ground as does the rain.
O Great Deity, you give splendor to the earth and sky. Hear
me, and place a luster on the echo of my words. Aho!

BANTER

The old New Mexican *santero* was carving a statue of the
Virgin Mary. "She must be beautiful beyond anything I have
ever carved," he said to his wife Annacita. "Yes," she agreed.
"It must be even more beautiful than your cedar angel, the one
you named *Ynocencia*. There is something in a name, old man."
"I feel that I am reaching the peak of my talent," he replied.
"By the way, old woman, what is it that you are cooking?
It smells so good." And the wife replied, "I feel that I am
reaching the peak of my talent. It is *posole*, my Christmas stew.
I have named it 'The *posole* of the snow falling on the barn
where Señora Diaz keeps her cat and seven kittens.'" "There is
something in a name," said the old *santero*.

THE BREATH OF THE INFINITE

It is a wind, they say, that blows from the dunes or the snowfields. And somewhere on the spectrum of its course there is a point. It is known to some, not many. There is a canyon, and in the canyon a crevasse. The walls are steep and vertical. At the far end of the crevasse the walls converge on the sky. At night the stars can be seen in a narrow ribbon at the zenith. Nowhere on earth are the stars brighter or more scintillant. And through the canyon on such a night there flows a silent wind. Just there is the point of time. There is drawn the breath of the infinite.

THROUGH A LENS OF COLD

An ice fog formed on the ground, and the man braced himself against the cold. His eyes blinked in the wind, and he struggled to keep upright and moving. He tried to conceive of summer, but the cold seemed all there was and had ever been. His mind began to buckle. Then, as he looked into the fog, the ice crystals seemed to form a ring, and in it a distance of sunlit green. There were bears in patches of berry bushes, and ravens cutting patterns on the bright air. And in the very center of the ring, Denali, the great mountain of the continent, looming in light. He imagined himself in the ring, and life returned to his body. Although the ring of crystals closed, he had seen beyond the real and immediate world into a season of deliverance, and he was no longer numb with cold.

THE GREEN STICK

Leo Tolstoy was born at Yasnaya Polyana, the family estate near Tula in Russia. He is buried there as well. In his will he wrote, "There should be no ceremonies while burying my body, a wooden coffin, and let anyone, who will be willing to, carry it to the *Stary Zakaz Wood*, near the ravine, to the place of the little green stick." It is said that when Tolstoy was a young boy he found the green stick and proclaimed that it was magical, that whoever should have possession of it could bring about peace in the world. The stick was lost, but Tolstoy, throughout his long life, believed in its power. It is the power of belief itself, perhaps, that he invested in the green stick. One who can muster that intensity of belief must be accorded attention and respect. For the sake of all souls imagine that the green stick lies near the ravine and near the mound where Tolstoy lies buried, waiting to be found. It is eminently worth the search, for it is the simple instrument of a child's profound faith. On the foundation of such a faith might world peace indeed be realized.

THE GHOST OF ADAM MEAGRE

The ghost appeared to me one night in a hotel in Santa Barbara. I had gone to bed and fallen asleep when something, something strange and sinister, awakened me. I beheld a vaporous form, then the shape of a man at the footboard. It frightened me, for it was menacing in its aspect. I felt a cold shiver on my skin. The next day I told a friend of what I had seen. "It was the ghost of Adam Meagre," I said. "How is it that you know his name?" my friend asked. "Oh, I named him," I replied. You see, there is power in names. I do not think that the ghost, Adam Meagre, knows my name, but I know his, having given it to him. I have the certain advantage of him. He can do me no harm, for he belongs to me.

CONFUSION

There is the case of a man who dreams he is a butterfly. Or is he a butterfly who dreams he is a man? And no doubt there are other possibilities. For example, what if Beowulf dreams he is Grendel or Grendel dreams he is Beowulf? I find this literary context more interesting because it admits of a whole story, regardless of who it is that dreams, and it has more of wonder and excitement about it. Tell me a story.

THE INTRUDER

On a sunny morning Elizabeth Bartram sat over coffee and scones in a corner of the veranda. She thought she heard voices from inside the house, but they were indistinct. A moment later an angel approached and greeted her with calm and goodwill. Strangely, she was not alarmed or even surprised to see such a figure. The angel was a young man of average appearance, except that he had large white wings, which he preened to good effect. He was rather handsome and pleasant in his demeanor. He apologized for having come through the house. "I thought you might be startled if I descended from the air," he said. Elizabeth was enchanted. "Why have you come?" she asked. "I have come to invite you to join our company, to be an angel." She was about to reply when the song of a bird awakened her. Later, on the veranda with coffee and scones, she wondered what it would be like to soar high above the earth. And just then a white feather came fluttering down from the sun and touched her shoulder.

TO A CHILD THIS GIFT

I would give you this,
The recognition of your innocence,
Your sacred being.
I would give you what delights you,
A ribbon, a taste of honey.
I would give you a seashell
And my hand to hold.
I would give you mornings in mist
And the sun setting on the sea.
I would give you kittens and puppies
And blackbirds over fields of snow.
I would give you songs and stories,
Calm and quiet in which to dream.
These gifts are one: the wish
That you take hold of the earth
Not as I have made it
but as you deserve it,
That you go in goodness
All the days of your life.

THE TYRANNY OF TIME

Time informs the universe. The structure of time is an enigmatic concept, a mystery that has challenged Man for as long as Man has existed. What is it? It is an infinite dimension in which we live our lives. It is an absolute condition of life itself. We do not know what it is; we know only *that* it is. It determines us. Commonly we think of time in terms of linear motion: time passes, time flies, time marches on, et cetera. But indeed we might postulate an opposite conviction, that time is static, and we move through it. The linear motion is ours. Consider a man in a raft on the Colorado River navigating the Grand Canyon. It is a wondrous experience, beautiful and nearly equal to the imagination. He is in a corridor of geologic time. He and the river move through it, not otherwise. We must take time for granted. There is no choice in the matter. With sophisticated instruments we take the measure of time, or think we do. In a kind of tyranny time explains us. We do not explain it. Is it tomorrow yet?

BLOOD MEMORY

The grandmother sat in her rocking chair. Her eyesight had grown weak, and she could no longer read. But she frequently kept an open book on her lap and *pretended* to read. She remembered stories that she had heard or read as a child, and she told them to her twelve-year-old grandson, Christopher. One day Christopher asked her to read to him from her book. "Oh, I will do better than that," she said. "I will tell you something that happened to me when I was your age. Well, a Black man who was known to us all as Cotton-Eye Joe used to come and pay a visit now and then. Oh, he was a *good-looking* man and he could *sing*! I tell you, that man could sing! As soon as he stepped on the porch he burst into song:

> *Well, I come for to see you, and I come for to sing,*
> *And I come for to show you my diamond ring.*

You know, Grandson, that was a long time ago, before the Civil War." "Wait a minute, Grandma. The Civil War was fought before you were born." She smiled. "The memory is in my blood. Cotton-Eye Joe would know what I mean."

IMPOSTURE

The case is famous. The essential facts are these: In 1548, Martin Guerre disappeared from his home in the village of Artigat in the Pyrenees, leaving his wife and son. In 1556 a man arrived in the village and claimed to be Martin Guerre. Many believed him, including members of the Guerre family, but some did not. Bertrande, Martin's wife, accepted the newcomer as her long-lost husband. Then one day an itinerant ex-soldier revealed the new Martin as an imposter. He said that he had served with Martin Guerre in the army and that Martin had lost a leg in battle. The accused man was identified as one Arnaud du Tilh, called "Pancette." Even at the trial there was much controversy. But a man entered the courtroom with a wooden leg and announced that he was Martin Guerre. Arnaud de Tilh was hanged in front of the Guerre house in Artigat. Beyond these facts are two untold stories: that of Pancette, whose nefarious skill and scheming are the stuff of dime novels, and that of Bertrande, the hapless victim of circumstances, whose heart must have withered and burned.

HANDPRINTS

In the cave of Gargas in the South of France there are some
five hundred negative handprints, placed there thousands
of years ago. Nearly half of them are missing digits. This is a
curiosity that has yet to be explained. Frostbite can be ruled
out, for the winter temperature in that region is moderate.
We know that among the tribes of the Great Plains of North
America it was once a practice to cut off fingers to signify
grief. But this too seems an unlikely explanation. It is however
possible that the cave dwellers of Gargas folded their fingers
in such a way as to eliminate them from the whole print of the
hand in order to convey some meaning in a sign language that
is unknown to us. It is fascinating to think that someone in
that time and place was perhaps taking an indispensable step
towards the formation of language as we know it.

THE PORTRAIT OF SPENCER KOHL

The late American artist James Reckert painted portraits of an abstract kind. He painted with acrylics on paper, and he worked quickly. He did not use models, and his portraits were not those of real people. Notwithstanding, he named them as if they were living souls. One of them, which he entitled, *A Portrait of Spencer Kohl*, is worth mentioning. It is the image of a round, bald head with blood red lips over uneven teeth and vacant white eyes. It might be considered a humorous, cartoonlike piece were it not for the fact that it is unarguably disturbing. Without exception, those who observe it are troubled by it, and they are glad to leave it behind. But Reckert thought of it as his best work. When asked why, he replied, "It speaks to me." This was taken to be a cliché until it was understood that he was being literal. The painting apparently spoke to him throughout the day, waking him in the morning, while shaving, during meals, even offering financial advice and tips on horse races. The whereabouts of the original painting is unknown. A copy hangs in the Breen Gallery in Chicago.

CROWS

From his room on the sixth floor he could see the courtyard below. And he could see the Lenin Hills, and beyond them the great city from which he felt estranged. It was a city of buildings, streets, parks, and people that, no matter how often he entered among them, he could never know. He was far from home, isolated. His loneliness was intense, and desperately he sought relief. Then one day as he looked out at the bleak sky and falling snow he saw the crows. They swirled down across his window and into the courtyard, busy it seemed, and noisy, as if they were gathering for some appointment, delegates to a convention of knaves. He was heartened to see them, for they signified a community of the familiar, and an old raucous music in the universe. In the droll presence of crows he was at home.

THE BURNING

At first there was smoke billowing, then the glow, then the flames. "Look, the cathedral is on fire!" The great building seemed to be standing apart from reality; it was vague, as in the interior of a dream. There was a general disbelief. But then there came a terrible confirmation. The spire fell. It did not dissolve or drop upon itself, but in what seemed slow motion, it leaned out, whole and flaming, and crashed down. The cathedral was destroyed. "It was a great monument to our spirit, and it must be restored." Overhearing this a woman prayed that the cathedral be remembered for what it was for hundreds of years. In that long time the cathedral had become a home of history, devotion, and national pride. One wonders what of these things, if any, might have gone up in flames, and what might be the challenge of such a restoration. Surely it is the challenge of faith itself.

A STONE FOR SINGING

She loved to sing, and she sang very well. But on this evening, the evening of the final rehearsal, her voice was not as strong as usual. Extensive travel had weakened her, and she went to the choirmaster with concern. He listened to her, then took her aside. He removed from his pocket a small, smooth stone and gave it to her. "Hold this in your hand when you sing, and keep your mind upon your hand." She was puzzled, but she did as he said. Her voice was strong and vibrant. Never had she sung so well. After rehearsal she asked the choirmaster if the stone were a crystal, for she knew that crystals were powerful. "No," he said, smiling. "It is just something I picked up in the road, a stone for singing." She had indeed kept her mind on the stone in her hand, and she had not been distracted. That seemed to her the likely explanation for her extraordinary performance, but she could not help wondering if there was magic in the stone. It was, after all, a stone for singing.

ONE HUNTER

The boy was half a centaur, and when he came of age he was given a spotted mare. There were embers in her eyes, and her muscles tensed and rippled in the sun. In one bound the boy mounted her and set her running. She ran faster and faster until the drumming of her hooves became one unbroken sound, and the boy felt his face slice the air, and the world became a blur of brilliant colors. One day they came upon a herd of buffalo grazing on the floor of a canyon, and they raced into the herd causing a stampede. The boy, riding with only his knees and heels, drew an arrow to his bow, but before he could release it, a great bull veered and hooked its massive head into them. The boy was gored in the leg and the mare in her shoulder. The boy fell heavily to the ground dazed and hurt, and the mare limped away. The boy was helpless and could not stand. But after a time the mare returned and lowered her head to him. He grasped her mane and she pulled him up and carried him home. In ceremony, an old man, once a centaur himself, gave them a single, powerful name, *One Hunter*.

THE EFFICACY OF PRAYER

The wife of Creeping Bear mourned the loss of her son, who had been slain on the Staked Plains. Every morning at sunrise she prayed that his journey beyond the earth should be safe and well provided. Creeping Bear chided her and said that her mourning must come to an end. She listened but could not overcome her grief. Then one night she was awakened by her son's voice, and he appeared to her in the light of embers. He was the tall handsome young man she remembered. "Mother," he said, "you have done right to pray for me. Your prayers have led me safely to the edge of the earth and beyond. There I am well and at peace. Of this I have come to assure you." And he was gone. The next morning Creeping Bear observed his wife at prayer and frowned in disapproval. But his wife turned a bright face to him and smiled.

THE ULTIMATE DREAM

He lay on the ground, mortally wounded. A friend wanted to remove him to a makeshift bed of blankets, but he refused. It was difficult for him to speak, but he spoke to his friend: You offer me comfort, and I am grateful, but I have only a little of life left, and I must spend it well. You see, this is the highest reach of my mortality. I am now face-to-face with my essential self, my soul. And I must own my soul at last, without help. I have lived on the earth, and I must die on the earth. I must now dream of the unknown. It is the ultimate dream, and I must enter it alone. I will be true to it.

A MORAL EQUATION IN ART

I wanted to get at the marrow of the bone, the essence of your deepest self. Only the black and white of a line drawing on paper would do. There must be the sharp clarity of contrast; color would dilute and disintegrate the one image that must emerge from the indefinite plane: you kneeling in an attitude of profound devotion, your closed eyes raised upward, closed but even so, deeply expressive, your throat long and lovely, your hair delineating the delicate curve of your shoulders, the perfect symmetry of your breasts. Above all I would have me attempt the mystical statement of your clasped hands, the lattice of their long, articulate fingers, interlocked in an elegance that exists in you alone and in the incomplete comprehension of my dreams. It may be that I can indicate these things in art, but I cannot render your center and your soul. So be it, the very intention, futile and arrogant, is not entirely without virtue.

FOREWARNED

Her first words to him were, "I am a witch." He appeared
to take this declaration in stride, but in fact he was caught
off balance, then delighted. She spoke in English but with a
pronounced accent which he took to be South African. He
invited her to dine with him that evening on the terrace of
the hotel in which, as it happened, both of them were staying.
She accepted, and they were seated at a table overlooking the
sea. The afternoon had been cloudy, but now the sky opened
to an infinite canopy of stars and a full moon that laid a trace
of bright light upon the water. She was beautiful, and he was
enchanted. Never had he been so drawn to a woman. As they
were having an after-dinner drink a man in a white jacket
approached them, and the woman introduced him as her
husband. "She is a witch," he said, and he bowed and departed.
The enchanted man was befuddled, and he returned to his
room. There he looked in a mirror and saw that he had grown
visibly older. The mirror shattered and left his image strewn in
a puzzle of shards on the floor. He was as it were dismembered
and could not remember himself.

MADNESS

In his last years Owen Chase began to hide food in the attic of his house. He was put away. As a young man he had served as first mate on the Nantucket whaler *Essex*. In 1820, some two thousand nautical miles off the coast of South America, the ship was rammed twice by a seemingly enraged sperm whale and sunk. The survivors, in three whaleboats on the open sea, suffered an unimaginable ordeal of dehydration, exposure, and starvation. In order to hold on to a thread of life they resorted to cannibalism. Chase must have had unspeakable dreams of the shipwreck, the aftermath, and perhaps especially the whale, the strange and terrible behavior of which cannot be explained. Herman Melville knew well the fate of the *Essex*, and he based *Moby-Dick* upon it. He might well have had Owen Chase in mind when he fashioned the character of the tormented and deranged Ahab. It is said that when the mind is so deeply wounded, madness sets in.

FACETS OF DISCOURSE

What of disorder, the rending of seams?
I dream of a day that has not come,
That dissolves not in fire but in memory:
The bright blending of morning and noon,
The glitter of leaves dancing, a flicker's wings.

Do you imagine a time of peace, even now
In the structure of discord and strife?
Are we not moored to history? We inherit
Challenge. We are driven hard to excel
As warriors excel, in fear and ferment.

Green meadows mark the rift of hills
Wherein clear waters flow, and hawks sail
Upon scented winds that bring crystal rain.
Ochre cliffs stand against the sun,
And a blue stillness holds upon the moon.

SUNRISE

The boy had seen the holy man at prayer, and he felt wonder
and fear in his heart. The holy man had prayed the sun up.
Every morning he had turned to the east, raised his arms, and
uttered the powerful words that made the sun rise. Then the
holy man died, and the boy suffered the pain and confusion
of loss. He turned to his father, who understood and said,
"The words of the holy man do not die. They keep his spirit
among us. His prayer remains on the wind, strong and
everlasting. The sun rose this morning, did it not?—and it
will rise tomorrow and the morning after. For this we must
give thanks to the holy man." Then the boy's heart was healed,
and from then on he gloried in the break of day.

THE WALL

He ran for the sheer exhilaration of running, but now he
was nearing the wall of his endurance. Somehow he must get
past the wall; he must run on the mere energy of his will. He
had started in the early morning when the first light slanted
on the skyline, and now it was nearly noon. A wave of pain
came over him, and he fought to overcome it. His whole
being was concentrated on the extreme edge of his effort. He
approached the wall, the limit of his tolerance that would
surely end his run. Then, in his peripheral vision he saw a dog
running beside him. The dog was beautiful, graceful, effortless
and fluent in its motion. It seemed to the runner to urge him
along. Together they ran, as if they were one entity, one force
of nature. There was a great burst of strength in him, and the
runner broke through the wall. At the end the runner looked
for the dog, but it was gone, and he realized that it might never
have been there at all. Nonetheless it remained in his mind as
an emblem of possibility, of the farthest reach within him.

A WOMAN'S VOICE

It was known to the people that a woman's voice had entered
into the holiest songs of the men's war society. It happened so:
From the time of the journey on the ice, the chosen men, those
who were priests and prophets, hunters and warriors, gathered
in a tent made of animal skins and sang prayers of ancient
origin. The songs were unintelligible, for they were sung in
the language of the mountain gods, and the people heard
them and accepted them as sounds that rang out from another
world and that nourished the sense of wonder. They were of
profound religious significance. Then one night, as there came
the singing of a sacred music, there was heard the voice of a
woman. It was beautiful and unmistakable. The people were
alarmed. When the war captains emerged from the tent, they
were fearfully confronted and they were astonished, for none
of them had heard a woman's voice. There was never a sign of
a woman's presence. The matter remains unresolved. It has
of course become a story, one that is taken to the heart. It is
a dream of itself.

THE CHILD'S DISCOVERY

There was a man who lived in Spain, in a region where there were prehistoric caves. He explored them and he found ancient paintings on the walls. One day he took his young daughter into a cave that he had visited a number of times before, a large cave of several chambers. Inside it was completely dark, and the man had to lead their way with a torch. Here and there he pointed to isolated paintings on the walls. They were relatively small and all in black. He explained that they were ancient, and his daughter was amazed. At last they came to a large room at the end of the cave. The man had never before observed the ceiling, and his daughter said excitedly, "Father, look up!" Above them was a large grouping of animals, nearly life-size and in vivid color. The man was speechless. There in the light of his torch was one of the greatest expressions of prehistoric art in the world. It had been preserved in total darkness. The man remained acutely aware of that moment. That the first person to behold this wonder in so many thousands of years was a child, *his* child, was an irony not lost upon him. He dreamed of it.

THE GRIEVER

He grieved, for he had lost one whom he loved more than his life. In his wretched state he went to an old blind woman who lived across the creek. From the time he was a small boy he had visited her when he sought to be comforted. He entered the room in which she sat huddled on the edge of her bed, rocking slightly back and forth, her sightless eyes frozen and open. His voice wavering, he said, "She is gone." He could say no more. There was a long silence, and then the old woman replied, "No. Her spirit remains, for I have seen it in the window." The man was perplexed, and as the night grew up around him he walked aimlessly through a wood, and he saw a point of light among the trees. There was a window, nothing else, and in the window a light. Peering, the man saw that a candle burned inside. The candle floated in the window, and the window floated in the darkness. There was nothing else. Spellbound, the man watched for a long time the flame guttering. And across the creek the old blind woman sat huddled on the edge of her bed gently rocking. For a moment her eyes seemed to reflect a glint of light.

THE WHIRLWIND

Platero was born crippled, and he was thrown away, for he was thought to be of no use. He was nearly helpless, but he managed to stay alive. In his youth he wandered in a desolate landscape. One day there came a whirlwind. It enveloped him and spun him to the ground. When he picked himself up he saw the world as he had not seen it before. No longer was the land desolate, but it had become in his vision beautiful. There was green growth all around and clouds and cliffs in sharp definition. There were brilliant colors and distances that ran to dark and mysterious mountains. And in Platero there was wonder. He became a great artist and the special pride of his people, those who had once abandoned him. In his old age he returned to the place of the whirlwind, and he made a prayer of thanksgiving to the earth.

THE READING

You hold the book in such a way that I think it must be very dear. Your voice is low, not quite the timbre of rain. My attention lags, but I see your hands, how they seem to caress the words as if they were the eggs of small birds or the fragile leaves of ancient papyrus—brittle, mythic texts. The room vibrates softly with your voice, like a metronome or the steady clock within me, the pulse of my imagination.

THE PIANO TEACHER

On the rainy afternoon of April 20, 1986, the piano teacher made her way to the Moscow Conservatory of Music. She was then an aged woman who lived alone, and she was in poor health, with only her piano and her few students to sustain her spirit. But today something of great importance was taking place. She had come to the conservatory to hear a performance by Vladimir Horowitz, who in his eighties had returned after a lifetime away to play a last time in his homeland. He took the bench to thunderous applause, and each of his selections was rendered flawlessly. It was an unforgettable performance. The piano teacher was enraptured, and her applause outlasted all the rest. Then Horowitz began to play Schumann's *Träumerei*. His fingers seemed not to touch the keys but to float above them, producing a melody so delicate as to be ethereal. She was so deeply moved that she could not applaud, for only the deepest silence of her soul was appropriate to this moment. She divined that she had seen and heard something as close to perfection as she would ever come, and tears came to her eyes.

WORLD RENEWAL

Based on pre-Columbian measurements of time thousands of years old, the world was expected to end in 2012. There were many believers, for the ancient calendars were known to have been time and again precisely accurate. And so it was in 2012. The world came to an end on schedule, but no one seemed to notice. The reason was this, according to a holy man who lived in the Sierra Madre mountains and who claimed to be of Aztecan descent. Long ago the people were divided by internal strife. A small band ventured to the north and became a self-sufficient people with their own system of customs and beliefs. Among their religious practices was one in which they reinvented the world. It happened, the holy man said, that the world renewal ceremony coincided with the end of the world. Indeed, one world ended and another was begun at exactly the same time. The transition was so smooth that it could not be perceived.

END NOTE

The landscape of words and dreams is vast. In the far distance are horizons that bank upon the heavens. The middle distance is a wilderness in which are the things that are barely within our reach, the oceans, mountains and forests, deserts and wildlife. And in the foreground are the properties of our daily lives, the neighborhood that is most familiar to us. And in the whole of this landscape is the intricate web of language and the imagination.

These sketches or "dream drawings," as I have named them, are furnishings of the mind. They are random and self-contained, and they are the stuff of story, and story is a nourishment of the soul. I have suggested elsewhere that there is only one story, that it is timeless and universal, and that it is composed of many stories in the one. That is true, I believe, and here are fragments of the original story, that which is told in the landscape of words and dreams.

ABOUT THE AUTHOR

N. Scott Momaday is an internationally renowned poet, novelist, artist, teacher, and storyteller. He is a member of the Kiowa tribe and has authored more than sixteen works that celebrate Native American culture and its oral storytelling traditions. In 1969 he won the Pulitzer Prize for his debut novel, *House Made of Dawn*—the first Native American to win the prize—and is the recipient of numerous awards and honors, including the 2021 Frost Medal for distinguished lifetime achievement in poetry, the Academy of American Poets Prize, a National Medal of Arts, the Anisfield-Wolf Lifetime Achievement Award, and the Dayton Literary Peace Prize Foundation's Ambassador Richard C. Holbrooke Distinguished Achievement Award. A longtime professor of English and American literature, Momaday earned his PhD from Stanford University and retired as Regents Professor at the University of Arizona. He lives in New Mexico.

READ MORE BY N. SCOTT MOMADAY

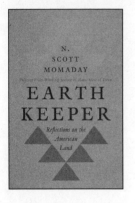

"Dazzling. . . . In glittering prose, Momaday recalls stories passed down through generations, illuminating the earth as a sacrosanct place of wonder and abundance. At once a celebration and a warning, *Earth Keeper* is an impassioned defense of all that our endangered planet stands to lose."
—*Esquire*

"These are the poems of a master poet. . . . When you read these poems, you will learn to hear deeply the sound a soul makes as it sings about the mystery of dreaming and becoming."
—Joy Harjo, Mvskoke Nation, U.S. Poet Laureate

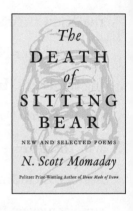

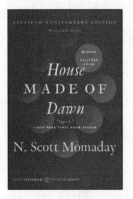

Winner of the Pulitzer Prize

"Both a masterpiece about the universal human condition and a masterpiece of Native American literature. . . . A book everyone should read for the joy and emotion of the language it contains."
—*The Paris Review*

"An intriguing combination of myth, fiction, and storytelling that demonstrates the continuing power and range of Momaday's creative vision. . . . These are magical words. Listen."
—*Washington Post*

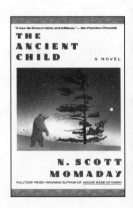

HarperCollins*Publishers* HARPER ● PERENNIAL